IT'S TIME TO EAT COTTAGE CHEESE

It's Time to Eat COTTAGE CHEESE

Walter the Educator

Silent King Books
A WhichHead Entertainment Imprint

Copyright © 2024 by Walter the Educator

All rights reserved. No part of this book may be reproduced in any manner whatsoever without written per- mission except in the case of brief quotations embodied in critical articles and reviews.

First Printing, 2024

Disclaimer

This book is a literary work; the story is not about specific persons, locations, situations, and/or circumstances unless mentioned in a historical context. Any resemblance to real persons, locations, situations, and/or circumstances is coincidental. This book is for entertainment and informational purposes only. The author and publisher offer this information without warranties expressed or implied. No matter the grounds, neither the author nor the publisher will be accountable for any losses, injuries, or other damages caused by the reader's use of this book. The use of this book acknowledges an understanding and acceptance of this disclaimer.

It's Time to Eat COTTAGE CHEESE is a collectible early learning book by Walter the Educator suitable for all ages belonging to Walter the Educator's Time to Eat Book Series. Collect more books at WaltertheEducator.com

USE THE EXTRA SPACE TO TAKE NOTES AND DOCUMENT YOUR MEMORIES

COTTAGE CHEESE

It's cottage cheese time, hooray, hooray!

It's Time to Eat Cottage Cheese

Soft and fluffy, white and whey!

In a bowl or on a spoon,

It's smooth and cool like a summer moon.

Little curds, so soft and round,

A tasty snack that's safe and sound.

Creamy, lumpy, fun to eat,

Cottage cheese is a yummy treat!

Plop, plop, scoop! It's fun to try,

With fruit or honey piled high.

Healthy and fresh from start to end,

Cottage cheese is our snacktime friend!

Packed with protein, soft and white,

It gives us strength with every bite.

Good for growing, bones, and play,

Cottage cheese helps us every day!

It's Time to Eat Cottage Cheese

With peaches, berries, or a pear,

Cottage cheese is beyond compare!

Add some veggies, or salt and spice,

It's the snack that's twice as nice!

Spread it on crackers, or eat it plain,

It's soft and light as summer rain.

A scoop, a dollop, or a heap,

It's the perfect snack before we sleep!

From creamy milk and dairy cheer,

Cottage cheese is mild and dear.

Soft and squishy, curds so small,

It's a snack that stands up tall!

For breakfast, lunch, or snacktime treat,

Cottage cheese is hard to beat!

In every spoonful, fresh and light,

It's Time to Eat
Cottage Cheese

It's the snack that's just right!

So let's all cheer, let's all say,

"Cottage cheese is here today!"

Healthy, yummy, soft, and bright,

It's cottage cheese time, let's take a bite!

Grab a spoon and let's dig in,

With cottage cheese, let's all begin!

Soft and creamy, fresh and fine,

It's Time to Eat

Cottage Cheese

The perfect snack, it's cottage cheese time!

ABOUT THE CREATOR

Walter the Educator is one of the pseudonyms for Walter Anderson. Formally educated in Chemistry, Business, and Education, he is an educator, an author, a diverse entrepreneur, and he is the son of a disabled war veteran. "Walter the Educator" shares his time between educating and creating. He holds interests and owns several creative projects that entertain, enlighten, enhance, and educate, hoping to inspire and motivate you. Follow, find new works, and stay up to date with Walter the Educator™ at WaltertheEducator.com

www.ingramcontent.com/pod-product-compliance
Lightning Source LLC
LaVergne TN
LVHW052011060526
838201LV00059B/3973